AN ABBEY THE
[WORLD

ABBEY THEATRE

PERVE

STACEY GREGG

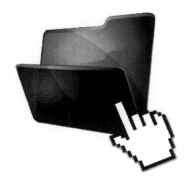

Premiered by the Abbey Theatre
on the Peacock stage on 31 May 2011.

The Abbey Theatre gratefully acknowledges the financial
support of the Arts Council / An Chomhairle Ealaíon.

This production will run without an interval.

CAST *(in order of appearance)*

Gethin	Ciarán O'Brien
Nick	Peter Campion
Lorraine	Andrea Irvine
Sarah	Roxanna Nic Liam
Taylor's Mum	Hilda Fay
Layla	Kerrie O'Sullivan
Authority	Jane Brennan

Director	Róisín McBrinn
Set Design	Alyson Cummins
Lighting Design	Aedín Cosgrove
Costume Design	Donna Geraghty
Sound Design	Denis Clohessy
Company Stage Manager	Stephen Dempsey
Deputy Stage Manager	Elaine Walsh
Assistant Stage Managers	Jean Hally
	Deirdre McClean
Voice Director	Andrea Ainsworth
Casting Director	Holly Ní Chiardha (CDG)
Hair and Make-up	Val Sherlock
Photographer	Johnny Savage
Sign Language Interpreter	Ali Stewart

AN ABBEY THEATRE COMMISSION

[WORLD PREMIERE]

ABBEY THEATRE

PERVE

STACEY GREGG

Perve by Stacey Gregg is an Abbey Theatre commission.

Perve is part of our published playscript series.
For further titles in the series please visit www.abbeytheatre.ie

Special thanks to Dr Judith McBrinn.

Please note that the text which appears in this volume may be
changed during the rehearsal process and appear in a slightly altered
form in performance.

ABBEY THEATRE
Amharclann na Mainistreach

The Abbey Theatre, Ireland's national theatre was founded by W.B. Yeats and Lady Gregory in 1904 to 'bring upon the stage the deeper thoughts and emotions of Ireland'. Since it first opened its doors, the Abbey Theatre has played a vital and often controversial role in the literary, social and cultural life of Ireland.

Over the years, the Abbey Theatre has nurtured and premiered the work of major playwrights such as J.M. Synge and Sean O'Casey as well as contemporary classics from the likes of Sebastian Barry, Marina Carr, Bernard Farrell, Brian Friel, Frank McGuinness, Thomas Kilroy, Tom Mac Intyre, Tom Murphy, Mark O'Rowe, Billy Roche and Sam Shepard. We continue to support new Irish writing at the Abbey through our commissioning process and our New Playwrights Programme.

The Abbey produces an annual programme of diverse, engaging, innovative Irish and international theatre. We place the writer and theatre-maker at the heart of all that we do, commissioning and producing exciting new work and creating discourse and debate on the political, cultural and social issues of the day. We connect with a new generation of theatre-goers through our Engage and Learn activities and through our popular Abbey Talks series.

In 1911 the Abbey Theatre first toured internationally. With a world-class reputation, the Abbey Theatre continues to tour taking on the role of an ambassador for Irish arts and culture worldwide.

Annie Horniman provided crucial financial support to the Abbey in its first years and many others have followed her lead by investing in and supporting our work. Now more than ever, we need support to ensure we continue to fuel the flame our founders lit over a century ago.

W.B. Yeats agus an Bantiarna Augusta Gregory a bhunaigh Amharclann na Mainistreach, amharclann náisiúnta na hÉireann, i 1904, d'fhonn na smaointe agus na mothúcháin ba dhoimhne de chuid na hÉireann a láithriú ar an stáitse. Riamh anall ón uair a d'oscail sí a doirse den chéad uair, bhí, agus tá, ról ríthábhachtach agus go deimhin, ról a bhí sách conspóideach go minic, ag Amharclann na Mainistreach i saol liteartha, sóisialta agus cultúrtha na hÉireann.

In imeacht na mblianta, rinne Amharclann na Mainistreach saothar mórdhrámadóirí ar nós J.M. Synge agus Sean O'Casey a chothú agus a chéadléiriú, mar a rinne sí freisin i gcás clasaicigh chomhaimseartha ó dhrámadóirí amhail Sebastian Barry, Marina Carr, Bernard Farrell, Brian Friel, Frank McGuinness, Thomas Kilroy, Tom MacIntyre, Tom Murphy, Mark O'Rowe, Billy Roche agus Sam Shepard. Leanaimid de thacaíocht a thabhairt do nuasríbhneoireacht na hÉireann in Amharclann na Mainistreach trínár bpróiseas coimisiúnúcháin agus ár gClár do Dhrámadóirí Nua.

Léiríonn Amharclann na Mainistreach clár amharclannaíochta as Éirinn agus ó thíortha thar lear in aghaidh na bliana atá ilghnéitheach, tarraingteach agus nuálach. Cuirimid an scríbhneoir agus an t-amharclannóir i gcroílár an uile ní a dhéanaimid, agus saothar nua spreagúil á choimisiúnú agus á léiriú againn agus dioscúrsa agus díospóireacht á chruthú i dtaobh cheisteanna polaitiúla, cultúrtha agus sóisialta na linne. Cruthaímid nasc leis an nglúin nua gnáthóirí amharclainne trínar ngníomhaíochtaí 'Téigh i ngleic leis agus Foghlaim' agus tríd an tsraith cainteanna dár gcuid a bhfuil an-tóir orthu.

I 1911 is ea a chuaigh complacht Amharclann na Mainistreach ar camchuairt idirnáisiúnta den chéad uair. Anois, agus cáil dhomhanda uirthi, leanann Amharclann na Mainistreach uirthi i mbun camchuairte agus í ina hambasadóir ar fud an domhain d'ealaíona agus cultúr na hÉireann.

Sholáthair Annie Horniman tacaíocht airgid ríthábhachtach don Mhainistir siar i mblianta tosaigh na hamharclainne agus lean iliomad daoine eile an dea-shampla ceannródaíochta sin uaithi ó shin trí infheistíocht a dhéanamh inár gcuid oibre agus tacaíocht a thabhairt dúinn. Anois thar aon am eile, tá tacaíocht ag teastáil uainn lena chinntiú go leanfaimid den lóchrann sin a d'adhain ár mbunaitheoirí breis agus céad bliain ó shin a choinneáil ar lasadh.

Writer, Creative Team & Cast

STACEY GREGG
WRITER

STACEY GREGG'S PREVIOUS work
at the Abbey Theatre includes
Cows Go Boom for the Abbey's
20:LOVE season and *Shibboleth*,
a co-commission with the Goethe
Institut and the Abbey Theatre
which had a reading directed by
Conall Morrison on the Peacock
stage as part of the Ulster Bank
Dublin Theatre Festival. Her first
play *Ismene* was shortlisted for
the Royal Court Young Writers
Festival. She was subsequently
on attachment at RADA, and
commissioned through Rough
Magic's SEEDS programme to
develop *Grand Tour*. She wrote
collaboratively for the Bush
Theatre London on *50 Ways to
Leave Your Lover* and Tinderbox
Belfast, for whom she is now
developing a further commission.
She was one of the playwrights
featured in Paines Plough's *Come
To Where I'm From* season. She is
currently on attachment with the
National Theatre Studio, and under
commission with Watford Palace
Theatre. Her devised production
Eveline Syndrome played at the
Dublin Fringe Festival. *Lagan* is
being currently being developed
with Root Theatre Company.
Stacey also writes for screen and is
developing an original television
series and a one off drama.

RÓISÍN MCBRINN
DIRECTOR

RÓISÍN PREVIOUSLY DIRECTED
No Escape and two plays in *The
Fairer Sex* at the Abbey Theatre.
Other productions include *Yerma*
in a new version by Ursula Rani
Sarma (West Yorkshire Playhouse),
Novecento (Donmar Warehouse@
Trafalgar Studios), *Station* and
Patroiophobia (Sherman Cymru),
Crestfall (Theatre 503), *The Field*
(Tricycle Theatre), *Tejas Verdes*
(b*spoke, Project Arts Centre),
Sleeping Beauty (Landmark,
Helix Theatre), *A Thousand
Yards* (Southwark Playhouse),
*References to Salvador Dali Make
Me Hot, Gompers* Arcola, *A is
for Axe* (Bewley's Café Theatre),
Sonnets for an Old Century and
Giants Have Us in Their Books
(Project Arts Centre). Róisín was
Resident Assistant Director at
the Donmar Warehouse in 2003.
She won the Young Vic Jerwood
Young Director's Award in 2004,
was director on attachment at the
National Theatre Studio in 2008

and was the recipient of the 2010 *Quercus Award* (in association with the National Theatre Studio and West Yorkshire Playhouse).

ALYSON CUMMINS
SET DESIGN

ALYSON PREVIOUSLY designed *No Escape* at the Abbey Theatre. She studied Architecture at UCD and after completing an internship at the Abbey Theatre she was awarded an Arts Council grant to train at the Motley Theatre Design School in London and was a finalist in the Linbury Biennial Prize for Stage Design 2007 on *Turandot* by Bertolt Brecht, directed by Tony Clarke for Hampstead Theatre. Other set designs include *The Trailer of Bridget Dinnigan* (ITM) and *Off Plan* (RAW, Project Arts Centre). Set and costume designs include *Hamlet* (Second Age), *The Colleen Bawn* (Project Arts Centre, Civic Theatre, Bedrock), *Serious Money, Dying City* (Rough Magic AIB SEEDS), *Extremities* (Spark to a Flame), *Crosswired* (East London Dance Festival and Shoreditch Festival), *The Trials of Brother Jero, Through a Film Darkly* (Arambe), *Daily Bread* (Dublin Youth Theatre), *Top Girls* (Galloglass),

Forget-me-not Lane (The Lit) and *Ya Get Me* (Old Vic education department). Alyson completed Rough Magic's AIB SEEDS programme during which she assisted designer Rae Smith on *The Birds* (Gate Theatre) and designer Monica Frawley on *I Puritani* (Nuremburg State Theatre), *The Giant Blue Hand* (The Ark) and *A Midsummer Night's Dream* (Opera Ireland). More recently she was assistant designer on the Gate Theatre's BPM Festival.

AEDÍN COSGROVE
LIGHTING DESIGN

AEDÍN'S PREVIOUS WORK at the Abbey Theatre includes *The Mai* by Marina Carr. She co-founded Pan Pan in 1991. Designs for Pan Pan include *Standoffish, Cartoon, MacBeth 7* (nominated for Best Lighting, Irish Times Theatre Awards 2004), *One: Healing with Theatre, Oedipus Loves You, The Idiots, The Playboy of the Western World* (Beijing), *The Crumb Trail* (nominated for Best Lighting, Irish Times Theatre Awards, 2009), *The Rehearsal Playing the Dane* at Dublin Theatre Festival 2010 (winner of the Irish Times Theatre Best Set Design Award and Best

Production 2010) and *Do Di Zhu* for Shanghai Dramatic Arts Centre and Shanghai Expo. Aedín travelled with director Sarah-Jane Scaife to Kuala Lumpur and Athens, where they produced *Come and Go, Rough for Theatre I, Act Without Words II, Footfalls* and *Nacht und Träume*. They also produced *Act Without Words II* at Absolut Fringe which was then presented at Dublin Theatre Festival 2010 as part of the Re-viewed programme. Aedín joined director Dylan Tighe to design lighting for *No Worst There Is None* in Newman House for the Dublin Theatre Festival and Junk Ensemble designing and lighting *Five Ways to Drown* which opened Dublin Dance Festival 2010. Earlier this year, she designed Set and Lighting for Opera Theatre Company's *Pasquale* and *Four Told* at Project Cube.

DONNA GERAGHTY
COSTUME DESIGN

DONNA IS A COSTUME assistant in the Abbey Theatre Costume Department. Her previous costume design work at the Abbey Theatre includes *No Romance* and *No Escape*. Other costume design credits include *Big Ole Piece of Cake* (Fishamble Theatre company), *The Townlands of Brazil* (Axis Theatre), *End Time, Playground and Olive Skin, Blood Mouth* (Gaiety School of Acting degree shows), *Red Light Winter, How To Act Around Cops and Shooters* (Purple Heart Theatre Company) and *One For Sorrow and Two For a Girl* (Skipalong Theatre Company). Donna is a graduate of the National College of Art and Design and Inchicore College of Further Education.

DENIS CLOHESSY
SOUND DESIGN

DENIS'S WORK AT the Abbey includes *The Rivals, The Resistible Rise of Arturo Ui, An Ideal Husband, Three Sisters, The Seafarer, Romeo and Juliet, The Crucible, Julius Caesar, Big Love, Burial at Thebes, Fool for Love* and *Woman and Scarecrow*. Other theatre work includes *Cat on a Hot Tin Roof, BPM, Death of a Salesman, Arcadia, Present Laughter, All My Sons, Faith Healer, The Yalta Game, The Real Thing, Hedda Gabler, Festen* (Gate Theatre), *The Importance of Being Earnest, Sodome, My Love, Solemn*

Mass for a Full Moon in Summer, Life is a Dream, Attempts on Her Life, Don Carlos (Rough Magic), *Hamlet, A Doll's House* (Second Age), *Happy Days, Cat on a Hot Tin Roof* (The Corn Exchange), *Silent, The Pride of Parnell Street* (Fishamble), *The Giant Blue Hand* (The Ark), *The Shawshank Redemption* (Lane Productions), *Macbeth* and *Titus Andronicus* (Siren Productions). This year Denis will be a participant in Rough Magic's *Advance* programme. Film work includes music for *His and Hers* (Venom Films), *Babyface Goes to Hollywood, A Bloody Canvas* and *The Long Arm of Dan Donnelly* (Fastnet Films). He has written the scores for numerous short films including *Undressing My Mother* and *Useless Dog* (Venom Films), for which he won Best Soundtrack at the 2005 European Short Film Biennale in Stuttgart. Television work includes *Gualainn le Gualainn* (Fastnet Film's history of Irish rugby) and the documentary series *The Limits of Liberty* (South Wind Blows) performed by the RTÉ Concert Orchestra.

JANE BRENNAN
AUTHORITY

JANE'S WORK AT the Abbey Theatre includes *No Escape, The Resistible Rise of Arturo Ui, The Burial at Thebes, Alice Trilogy* (for which she received an Irish Times Theatre Award for Best Actress), *The Crucible, Footfalls, The Last Apache Reunion, A Crucial Week in the Life of a Grocer's Assistant, The Playboy of the Western World, The Secret Fall of Constance Wilde* (Melbourne Arts Festival and The Barbican), *The Wake* (International Edinburgh Festival), *The House, Saint Joan, The Rivals, Dancing at Lughnasa, Bailegangaire* and *Homebody*. Other theatre work includes *Jane Eyre, Pygmalion, Pride and Prejudice, One for the Road, Not I*, Beckett Festival, Lincoln Center, New York (Gate Theatre), *'Tis Pity She's a Whore, Loot, A Little Like Drowning, Conversations on a Homecoming, The Singular Life of Albert Nobbs, The Beauty Queen of Leenane*, Duke of Yorks, London (Druid), *Digging for Fire, Spokesong, The Way of the World, The Sugar Wife*, Soho Theatre, London (Rough Magic) *Far Away* (Bedrock) and *Splendour*

(RAW). Jane is a co-founder of b*spoke Theatre Company where she appeared in *Electra, Boston Marriage* and *Tejas Verdes* and produced *The Drunkard, Family Stories, Hysteria* and *The Sanctuary Lamp*. Radio includes *Three Sisters, The Plough and the Stars* and *The Trojan Women*. Film and television credits include *Fair City, Black Day at Black Rock, Benedict Arnold, The Clinic, Intermission, Studs, Perrier's Bounty, Single-Handed II* and *The Tudors*. Jane is a member of the Abbey Theatre Board.

PETER CAMPION
NICK

THIS IS PETER'S FIRST TIME working at the Abbey Theatre. His theatre credits include *The White Guard* (National Theatre, London). Television credits include *Raw* and *Love / Hate* (RTÉ). Peter trained at the Guildhall, London.

HILDA FAY
TAYLOR'S MUM

HILDA'S LAST APPEARANCE at the Abbey Theatre was in *Little Gem* (Gúna Nua) and *The Playboy of the Western World*. Her theatre work includes *Little Gem*, for which she received Best Actress Award, Dublin Fringe 2008 (Project Arts Centre, Civic Theatre, Olympia, Flea Theatre, New York and the Traverse, Edinburgh where it won The Best of Edinburgh Award 2009), *The Vagina Monologues* (Tivoli Theatre, national tour), *The Woman Who Walked into Doors* (Olympia, Helix), *Fontamara, Green* (Vesuvius), *Kiss 'n' Tell* (Andrews Lane), *Aladdin, Sinbad, Cinderella* (Gaiety Theatre), *An Feilican Fan* (Crypt) and *Trojan Woman* (Plush). Film and television credits include *Finbar's Class, Ordinary Decent Criminal, Saltwater, Though the Sky Falls, Proof, Prosperity, On the Street Where You Live, The Clinic* and *Whistleblower,* for which she was nominated for an IFTA for Best Supporting Actress. Hilda is best known to the Irish public for her role as Tracey in *Fair City*. She graduated from the Bachelor in Acting Studies course at the Samuel Beckett Centre, Trinity College.

ANDREA IRVINE
LORRAINE

ANDREA'S PREVIOUS WORK at the Abbey Theatre includes *The East Pier, Macbeth, Terminus, The Bacchae of Baghdad, The Wild Duck, The House of Bernarda Alba, Down the Line, Macbeth, Angels in America, The Crucible, A Woman of No Importance* and *In a Little World of Our Own*. Other theatre work includes *Life is a Dream, The Bonefire, The Whisperers, Pentecost, The Way of the World, Love and a Bottle* (Rough Magic), *The Real Thing, Hedda Gabler, Anna Karenina, Poor Beast in the Rain, Dancing at Lughnasa, A Christmas Carol* (Gate Theatre), *Women in Arms* (Storytellers), *Our Lady of Sligo* (Out of Joint, National Theatre, London), *Roberto Zucco, Massacre@Paris* (Bedrock Productions), *Cruel and Tender* (Hatch), *Wonderful Tennessee, Skylight* (Lyric Theatre, Belfast), *Judith* (Open Door), *Speed the Plow* (Project Arts Centre), *Antigone* (Druid), *King Lear* (Second Age) and *Bold Girls* (7:84 Scotland). Film and television credits include *Five Minutes of Heaven, The Clinic, Evelyn, Ella Enchanted, Gold in the Streets, Ailsa, DDU / Making the Cut, Sensation, Wild Decembers* and the soon to be released, *Stella Days*.

ROXANNA NIC LIAM
SARAH

ROXANNA RECENTLY appeared in *The Passing* by Paul Mercier at the Abbey Theatre. Other theatre credits include *Paper Boy and Friends, THEATREclub Stole Your Clock Radio What The Fuck You Gonna Do About It?, Rough* (THEATREclub), *Complexity* (The Complex), *Daily Bread, This is Still a Life, The Cripple of Inishmaan* (Project Arts Centre) and *City Breaks* (Dublin Fringe). Film credits include *Agnes Brown* and *The General*. She recently starred in the short film *Two Hearts* (Calipo Productions).

CIARÁN O'BRIEN
GETHIN

CIARÁN'S WORK AT the Abbey Theatre includes Winterbottom in *Arrah-na-Pogue*, Corporal Stoddart in *The Plough and the Stars,* Dromio of Ephesus in *The Comedy of Errors*, Inna and Young Dogsborough in *The Resistible Rise of Arturo Ui*, Colin in *Saved*, Lucius in *Julius Caesar* and *The Importance of Being Earnest*. Other theatre work includes Ronan in Ross O'Carroll Kelly's *Between Foxrock and a Hard*

Place (Gaiety Theatre and Cork Opera House), Tommy in *The Shawshank Redemption* (Gaiety Theatre, Cork Opera House, Derry Millennium Forum), Gar Public in *Philadelphia, Here I Come!* (Gaiety Theatre), Crawford in *Observe The Sons of Ulster Marching Towards the Somme* (Livin Dred, Nomad), Warren in *This is Our Youth* (Bedrock Productions), John and Smee in *Peter Pan* (Pavilion Theatre), Lenny in *The Magic Tree* (Granary Theatre, Edinburgh Fringe, Belltable Theatre, Dublin Fringe), Sk8er Jack in *Lil' Red and Sk8er Jack* (Civic Theatre), 1 in *Fewer Emergencies* (Randolph SD | The Company), Jerry in *How Many Miles to Babylon?* (Second Age), chorus in *Myrmidons* (Oroborus), Warren in *Seven Deadly Teens* (Dublin Fringe) and Artful Dodger in *Oliver Twist* (Gate Theatre). Television and film credits include *The Last Security Man* (RTÉ Storyland), *The Tudors, Fair City, Detained, Bloom, Prince William, Fear, Custer's Last Stand Up* and *The Boy from Mercury*. Ciarán is a graduate of Bachelor of Acting studies, Samuel Beckett Centre Trinity College.

KERRIE O'SULLIVAN
LAYLA

KERRIE LAST APPEARED at Abbey Theatre in *By the Bog of Cats* when she was a small child. She graduated from the Bachelor in Acting Studies course at the Samuel Beckett Centre, Trinity College. Productions while in training include *The Winter's Tale, The Cherry Orchard, Sweeney Astray, The Drunkard, Now is the Winter of our Discontent* and *Hot Fudge*. Other theatre work includes *Skin and Blisters* (TEAM), *The Hostage* (Wonderland Productions), *A Christmas Carol* (Gate Theatre) and her dance credits include *Beckett Embodied* (Smurfit Business School). Film and television work includes *The Tudors* (Showtime), *Ten Steps* (SP Films), *Fair City* and *No Tear* (RTÉ).

Next at the Abbey Theatre ...

23 JUNE – 13 AUGUST 2011
TRANSLATIONS
Brian Friel

23 AUGUST – 10 SEPTEMBER 2011
CURSE OF THE STARVING CLASS
Sam Shepard

21 SEPTEMBER – 5 NOVEMBER 2011
JUNO AND THE PAYCOCK
Sean O'Casey

CO-PRODUCTION BETWEEN THE ABBEY THEATRE AND
THE NATIONAL THEATRE OF GREAT BRITAIN

24 NOVEMBER 2011 – 21 JANUARY 2012
THE GOVERNMENT INSPECTOR
Nikolai Gogol
in a new version by
Roddy Doyle

PERVE

Stacey Gregg

Characters

GETHIN, *twenty-three*
NICK, *twenty-two*
LORRAINE, *Gethin and Sarah's mum*
SARAH, *sixteen*
TAYLOR'S MUM
LAYLA, *eighteen*
AUTHORITY

Note on the Text

A forward slash (/) in the text indicates the point at which the next speaker interrupts.

A word in brackets is usually thought but not spoken.

Whole lines in brackets indicate the less dominant voice in ongoing and overlapping dialogue.

This text went to press before the end of rehearsals and so may differ slightly from the play as performed.

Scene One

A graffitied house.

'Pervert' and 'GET OUT' scrawled across, paint splats.

GETHIN, *bright and charismatic, sits on a wall, fiddling with a video camera on a tripod. Beside him sits* NICK, *genial, drinking from a can. They have the easy banter of old mates.*

NICK *watches him fiddle for a few moments.*

NICK	reckon Spielberg started like this?
	GETHIN *ignores him.*
	Gethin, d'ya reckon / Spielberg started like this –
GETHIN	(*Concentrating.*) Shut up
	NICK *sniggers, takes a slug from the can.*
	Looks bored.
NICK	Hurry up, mate, we'll miss the match
GETHIN	We won't, chill out.
	I just want a few shots…
NICK	Shag marry kill: Spielberg, Scorsese, Tarantino
GETHIN	Spielberg, he's the best. Easily.
NICK	mmm.
	I liked *E.T.*
GETHIN	See *Schindler's List*?
	NICK *screws up his face.*
NICK	Nah, not my cuppa tea.
	Hah – 'not my cuppa tea', '*E.T.*'

GETHIN	the Holocaust isn't your cuppa tea?
NICK	nah.
	Who would you shag –
GETHIN	don't know
NICK	– Tarantino all the way.
GETHIN	Tarantino?
NICK	by a mile. Pass the soap – oh Quentin!

GETHIN breaks a smile.

GETHIN	So, like, watching a film about the Holocaust is worse than watching – I don't know – the same old Tarantino torture shit, like, women with guns attached to their limbs?
NICK	Yeah but it's cool
GETHIN	cretin.

It's NICK's turn to scoff.

NICK	*Schindler's List*... pft.
	Came on TV, over Christmas, and it was like boohoohoo BANG face blown off a small child and Mum switched it over. Like, Mum doesn't even watch the news. On principle. Says she doesn't want to see any wickedness, there's enough wickedness in the world. She reckons that's why people get the depression, watching too much news.
GETHIN	it's a stunning movie
NICK	stunningly depressing
GETHIN	Fellini is the all-time best
NICK	Fellatio. Panini.
GETHIN	I'm not gonna bite
NICK	what's that supposed to mean?
GETHIN	I mean you're winding me up

NICK	no I'm not
GETHIN	and I'm above it, mate
NICK	mate, I don't premeditate my small talk with the sole intention of winding you up, I've better things to think about.
	Like chips. And a cold pint. A cold pint of / beeeeeer
GETHIN	okay, God.
	GETHIN *starts recording*.
NICK	So what's it for?
	A Gethin Spotlight Special.
	'Paedos on the Run'
GETHIN	Yep
NICK	'Paedos on Ice'
GETHIN	Yep
NICK	'Stars in Your Paedo'
GETHIN	yep
NICK	'Paedo Swap'
GETHIN	yep
NICK	'I'm a Perve, Get Me Out of Here'?
GETHIN	Good for you, admitting it, Nick, after all these years.
NICK	only thanks to your mum.
	Beat.
	So what is it? What's it for?
GETHIN	don't know yet. Just an idea. A concept, you know
NICK	ooh a 'concept'
	GETHIN *finally has the camera set*.

He steadies and takes a shot of the damage.
The graffiti.

GETHIN   No one ever gets done for this crap.

I mean, that's vandalism really.

Beat.

NICK   Why don't you make a nice film about a guy
who falls in love with a girl, but he doesn't
know he likes her cos she wears big glasses
and looks like a nerd, but then, one night of
pure passion she / takes off the glasses

GETHIN   let me guess, she / takes off the glasses –

NICK   And in the bedroom she's a total dominatrix, /
and –

GETHIN   Nah.

NICK   what?!

GETHIN   Been done.

NICK   Not enough. Never enough.

NICK *mimes swishing his hair.*

(*Movie voice.*) 'Of course I'll help you with
your library card, sir'

GETHIN   besides, that's like, fiction. Real life's much
weirder.

NICK   I'll tell you what's weird. Two guys sitting
outside a perve's house perving on him with a
video camera.

GETHIN   he's not even a perve

NICK   What?

GETHIN   (*A shrug.*) I mean, we don't know that.
Necessarily.

NICK   he is

GETHIN   you don't know

NICK	there's a fair consensus
GETHIN	there were no charges, so…
NICK	yeah but no smoke without fire
GETHIN	habeas corpus
NICK	Your what's itchy?
GETHIN	my balls – innocent till / proven guilty
NICK	why're you defending him?
GETHIN	I'm not
NICK	you are
GETHIN	I'm not 'defending him'
NICK	you are
GETHIN	I'm not *defending* – just wonder when it became like, guilty until proven innocent.
	Like, what if he *is* innocent. Like, all these guys out there that've been accused of rape or abuse and then the allegations turn out to be false, you're always reading about it, and their lives are totally screwed up. That's it for them. I mean, surely that's crueler than –
NICK	child abuse itself? Yeah see what you mean there – good point
GETHIN	that's not / what I was –
NICK	sick, sicko bastard
GETHIN	fuck, see?
NICK	see what
GETHIN	exactly what I mean
NICK	for someone who's such a brainybox
GETHIN	everyone's so hysterical, get so hysterical – just takes one person to / throw a stone
NICK	I'll tell you what makes me hysterical

GETHIN	then it's paint and graffiti / and lynching
NICK	– you faffing about on that camera when the match is about to start
GETHIN	*okay*
NICK	Can we go now?
GETHIN	Yes.
	Philistine
NICK	I know you are
GETHIN	Alright fine, whatever.

GETHIN *closes down the shot.*

NICK	Got what you needed?
GETHIN	yep. Let's go!
NICK	woo

GETHIN *switches off the camera and* NICK *gives a hand, jangling his car keys as they go.*

NICK *is singing a football song joyfully.*

GETHIN *catches a glimpse of something.*

GETHIN	wait –
NICK	what?
GETHIN	think I just saw him, at the window
NICK	what, paedo Bob?
GETHIN	yeah.
NICK	where?
GETHIN	Y'know he was a caretaker
NICK	bet he was
GETHIN	at a school
NICK	(*Paedo voice.*) 'like a sweetie from my pocket?'
GETHIN	and has like, learning difficulties

NICK	whatever
GETHIN	that's what I heard. Just sayin'.
	Poor bastard.
NICK	fuck, d'you want to go and make friends with him or wha'? Play a quick game of table tennis together? Cos I'm goin to the pub now, okay?
GETHIN	yeah, I'm coming, it's my round.

They leave, messing about.

Scene Two

Evening.

GETHIN*'s bedroom.*

GETHIN *on the internet.*

His finger hovers over the mouse.

He is on the brink of clicking.

His hand withdraws, suspended.

LORRAINE	(*From the kitchen.*) GETHIN! DIN-NER!
	GETHIN *is startled, edgy.*
GETHIN	Coming
LORRAINE	I'VE ALREADY CALLED YA

Behind him, SARAH peeps into his room. She squints to see what GETHIN is doing.

GETHIN *turns back to the screen.*

Impulsively clicks in.

He looks immediately disgruntled and clicks out again.

SARAH *is shocked, and then delighted.*

She scuttles off. GETHIN *spins round at the noise.*

GETHIN   – Sarah?

LORRAINE   GETHIN!

GETHIN   OKAY!

GETHIN shuts his laptop and goes.

Scene Three

Dinner table. GETHIN, LORRAINE *and* SARAH *sit around the table eating.*

SARAH   You so are

GETHIN   I'm so not

SARAH   Oh my God, you so are

GETHIN   I'm so not

SARAH   you ARE

GETHIN   Mum

LORRAINE   (*Autopilot.*) Sarah, Gethin is not a psychopath.

SARAH   Mum, you've no idea

LORRAINE   I've got lots of ideas –

SARAH   Mum, seriously

LORRAINE   He just likes to read more than you and work in his room and get some peace, which is something I'd quite like myself, so Shut Up and Eat Your Dinner.

             They eat for a moment, subdued.

SARAH   Alright, maybe not a psychopath but he is so a perve

LORRAINE	That's enough, Sarah
SARAH	Mum'll kill you
GETHIN	I'm twenty-three, don't think she will
LORRAINE	No age is too old for a slap.
SARAH	You'll get a slap!
GETHIN	Can you pass the salt?
SARAH	I *can*.

She doesn't.

LORRAINE	What's wrong with you, you're nearly dead to tell on him
SARAH	He's been looking at paedos on the internet, making friends with them
GETHIN	Sarah, shut up
LORRAINE	What?
SARAH	I saw him
GETHIN	I wasn't 'making friends'
SARAH	pfft
GETHIN	I was researching
LORRAINE	What kind of research?
GETHIN	research
SARAH	'research'
LORRAINE	What for?
GETHIN	Exactly this. How people freak out. Don't worry, Mum, you can't catch perve-itus.
LORRAINE	You know they monitor what you're looking at
GETHIN	Mum, please don't try to understand the internet, you'll hurt yourself.
LORRAINE	I'm not laughing, Gethin.

GETHIN	'They' don't monitor. That's half the point.
LORRAINE	Well, what research is it? Your course finished, didn't it?
GETHIN	no, it's just for – I'm just researching how everyone goes crazy at the 'P' word.
(SARAH	palaeontology?)
GETHIN	– it's like this hysteria in the western world.
SARAH	ooh 'I did a course in film studies ooooh'
LORRAINE	Sarah
SARAH	what?
GETHIN	and you know how many people's lives it's ruined? There was a paediatrician who got hounded out of their town because people confused the word with paedophile! But nobody would back down or / apologise
LORRAINE	You can't defend those monsters
GETHIN	they're people, not 'monsters'
SARAH	seriously, Mum, not all paedos are bad, some of my best friends are paedos
GETHIN	statistically the abusers were often abused themselves, so at what point do they become 'monsters'
SARAH	at what point does Gethin's head disappear entirely up his own arse?
LORRAINE	Sarah! – Gethin –
GETHIN	They have rights. And some are innocent, loads are rehabilitated
LORRAINE	Gethin
GETHIN	What?
LORRAINE	I don't want you doing – what are you doing?
	What's it for?

GETHIN   An experiment. And I'll make a documentary
                out of it or something. (*Delighted with
                himself.*) 'Exploding Taboos' or somethin'

                LORRAINE *tuts.*

                Mum, don't you think that –

LORRAINE   I don't want to hear any more about it

GETHIN   cos that's a great argument

LORRAINE   Give over being a smart-arse

GETHIN   but Mum

LORRAINE   No.

GETHIN   Mum

LORRAINE   NO

GETHIN   but I just want the salt

SARAH   what's pederasty?

LORRAINE   *What?*

SARAH   that's another 'P' word

                LORRAINE *passes the salt and sighs.*

                They eat on in silence.

                LORRAINE *pours herself some more tea.*

LORRAINE   Have you finished that wedding film for Kelly
                and Adam yet?

                GETHIN *pulls a face.*

                Have you?

GETHIN   It's in post-production

LORRAINE   So no. Well, can you please get that done
                before you go off doing whatever else?
                They'll be divorced by the time you actually
                finish it. And remember they want Wet Wet
                Wet over the wedding vows, 'I feel it in my
                fingers'

SARAH	(*Sings to herself*.) 'I feel it up my no-ose'
LORRAINE	Sarah, love, go and feel the washing up
SARAH	uuuGHGHH ALRIGHT FINE I'M NOT ALLOWED TO EXPRESS MYSELF NOW

SARAH *departs*.

LORRAINE	(*Quietly*.) I don't want to hear any more about it, okay.

LORRAINE *lifts her own dishes and leaves*.

Scene Four

Morning.

SARAH *in her school uniform, cleaning toothpaste from her tie*.

GETHIN *sitting in shorts with a coffee, watching television*.

SARAH *tuts*.

GETHIN	toothpaste again?
SARAH	get a job
GETHIN	I'm fine, thanks
SARAH	you're such wanker
GETHIN	you're so fat
SARAH	I hate you
GETHIN	Trish or *GMTV*?
SARAH	Trish

GETHIN *flicks the channel*.

Beat.

They watch, content.

GETHIN	Shouldn't you've gone?

SARAH	I can actually wait till twelve minutes past before I go and I'll still make it actually
GETHIN	okay.
	Don't blame me when you're late.
SARAH	don't blame me when you're retarded
GETHIN	loser
SARAH	it's Dad's birthday this weekend
GETHIN	so
SARAH	just remindin' you.
GETHIN	as if I care. As if I'm going to, like, send a little card. 'Happy birthday Daddy! How's the whore?' Whatever.
SARAH	ohmyGod you're so gay
GETHIN	shouldn't say that
SARAH	duh, don't mean you're actually homosexual, I just mean you're, like, crap
GETHIN	yeah you couldn't use an ethnic slur the same way, could you? Couldn't call something crap 'black', could you?
SARAH	OhmyGod, can't believe you said that
GETHIN	I didn't say that. I said you couldn't call something crap 'black'. So you shouldn't call something crap 'gay'. You're gay, ya twat
SARAH	I'm so tellin'
GETHIN	you're so late, it's thirteen minutes past
SARAH	OhmyGod, you did that on purpose!
GETHIN	changed the pace of time? Yes, I did that.
SARAH	You are such an unemployed perve.
	SARAH *throws everything sitting around into her bag and tries to tie her hair up and find her bus pass all at the same time.*

I'm gonna tell people you're a weirdo perve
who looks up perves on the internet

GETHIN   like to see ya try

GETHIN absorbs this, however, and looks at her.

SARAH   You can star in your own stupid documentary

GETHIN   I'd watch that

SARAH   so would I, you and paedo BOB

GETHIN   What, like evidence in action

SARAH   'Sarah's Story: Living with a Perve'

GETHIN   and I could show how vicious people are –
forget Bob, that'd be an amazing premise

GETHIN dismisses the idea…

But the more he thinks about it…

He sits up a fraction.

would you actually?

SARAH   what?

GETHIN   would you? Do that for me?

SARAH stops, and looks at him.

He's serious.

SARAH   WHAT. YOU'RE SO WEIRD WHERE'S MY
BUS PASS

GETHIN   under your tampons, there

SARAH   SHUDDUP

SARAH snatches up the contents of her bag.

GETHIN   Tell people at school I'm a perve. Go on. See
what happens.

SARAH   what?

*She has collected up her stuff, and stands,
ready to make an exit.*

GETHIN   go on. You'll be a natural at it.

SARAH   how'd you mean?

GETHIN   For my project. You know, about how
            ridiculous people are. Just start a rumour and
            see what happens...

SARAH   about you?

GETHIN   yeah.

SARAH   but you *are* a perve

GETHIN   well then

            SARAH *weighs him up: what's the catch?*

SARAH   gonna pay me?

GETHIN   Sarah, how many times in your life are you
            gonna get licence to talk shit about me? You
            should be payin' me.

SARAH   Cool. Okay.

GETHIN   cool

SARAH   talk shit about you. No probs.

GETHIN   Here –

            GETHIN *picks up and passes* SARAH *her
            crisps she's forgotten.*

            have a lovely day, shithead

SARAH   thanks, dickbitch

            SARAH *races out the door.*

            GETHIN *mutes the TV.*

            *He picks up his video camera and puts it on the
            tripod.*

            Aims it at himself.

            Clears his throat.

Scene Five

The kitchen. LORRAINE *is washing the dishes,* TAYLOR'S
MUM *sits at the dinner table, flicking through a magazine.*

LORRAINE   so he says to her that he'd heard it makes oral
                  sex so much better

TAYLOR'S MUM   humming

LORRAINE   right – when you're down there, you should
                  hum, so he says to her that night, they're

TAYLOR'S MUM   – gettin' jiggy

LORRAINE   right – he says, 'have you thought any more
                  about that thing I mentioned?'

TAYLOR'S MUM   that thing

LORRAINE   that 'thing.' And she's like, 'oh right, do you
                  want me to…?'

TAYLOR'S MUM   right!

LORRAINE   you know, and he says 'yeah, sure, where's the
                  harm.' So she's down there, doing that, and –
                  the way he tells it, God – she looks up at him –
                  you should see how he tells it –

                  LORRAINE *mimes holding a penis in one
                  hand near her mouth, like a microphone.*

                  and she looks up at him and says – 'any
                  requests?'

                  They cackle.

TAYLOR'S MUM   'Any requests!'

                  LORRAINE *blows into the microphone penis.*

LORRAINE   One two. One two. Testing.

SARAH *appears in the kitchen. The women bubble down.*

SARAH   what are you laughing at?

TAYLOR'S MUM   your mum said something funny

SARAH   well, that's a lie

TAYLOR'S MUM   about microphones

SARAH   right.

                 SARAH *pours herself some juice.*

                 Beat.

TAYLOR'S MUM   How's you?

SARAH   so-so

                 Silence.

                 SARAH *leaves, somehow communicating her existential disdain.*

TAYLOR'S MUM   hope you don't mind me saying, Lorraine, but I just dread when Taylor gets to that age.

LORRAINE   I know. They aren't totally without charm, but you do forget it's there, under all the mascara and cheek and doors slamming.

TAYLOR'S MUM   well, hopefully Taylor'll skip the mascara.

LORRAINE   hopefully!

TAYLOR'S MUM   Though he was always partial to my kitten heels.

LORRAINE   but what legs for a seven-year-old boy

TAYLOR'S MUM   Oh dear. For shame.

                 I knew though, I knew we shouldn't have given him a feminine name.

LORRAINE   Taylor's not feminine, is it?

TAYLOR'S MUM   it is feminine

LORRAINE   Taylor?

TAYLOR'S MUM   it is now, Lorraine, there's at least four girls at his school called Taylor – Taylor Lammy, Taylor Breen, Taylor Naylor –

LORRAINE   Taylor Naylor?

TAYLOR'S MUM   well, I don't know, I can't remember the other two, but there's definitely four, and there's definitely a Lammy and a Breen

LORRAINE   yeah but that's the fashion now, with names –

TAYLOR'S MUM   mm suppose

LORRAINE   unisexual or something

TAYLOR'S MUM   well. Tom's not convinced. He still brings it up.

LORRAINE   yeah but Tom's idea, what was it again –

TAYLOR'S MUM   Tyson

LORRAINE   Tyson!

TAYLOR'S MUM   could you imagine

LORRAINE   and with how gentle he's turned out

TAYLOR'S MUM   (*Nettled.*) 'gentle'?

LORRAINE   well, y'know, I just mean, it might've been hard to… grow into – 'Tyson' – it's very – *rar*, y'know? Like imagine if you called your baby girl Grace and she turned out to be a wee fatty, always knocking things over – it's risky

TAYLOR'S MUM   no I know. Think Tom reckons the name is half the reason, though. Like if we'd called him a tough name he'd've had to fill it.

LORRAINE   Oh, I don't think so

TAYLOR'S MUM   Well. He's only seven. Kids change.

LORRAINE *looks at her friend.*

LORRAINE   You're not, worried –

TAYLOR'S MUM   Life's too short. He'll be fine. Tom'll be
                 fine. He's just funny, Tom, old-fashioned in his
                 own way. He's a real thing about the
                 importance of father figures, and how much of
                 an effect it has on kids, boys especially – oh –
                 sorry, Lorraine – I didn't / mean –

LORRAINE   Christ, no

TAYLOR'S MUM   I just mean

LORRAINE   don't worry. Course. Lots of people do. But it's
                 not like I had the choice. And I honestly don't
                 think Gethin or Sarah have gone without
                 anything other kids've had.

TAYLOR'S MUM   course.

LORRAINE   and he left them. So.

TAYLOR'S MUM   (*Dutiful.*) bastard

LORRAINE   well.

                 Whole clan of them.

TAYLOR'S MUM   ever hear from him? Or Rory?

LORRAINE   (*Subdued.*) God no.

                 Don't even think they're in contact with each
                 other.

TAYLOR'S MUM   Do you know where Rory's livin'?

LORRAINE   (*Deliberately changing the topic.*) Think you'll
                 have more? Kids?

TAYLOR'S MUM   (*Taking the hint.*) Maybe. Maybe I will. I
                 don't want to leave it much later. Don't know
                 how Tom would feel. There's so much needing
                 done to the house at the moment though – I
                 must remember, Nick's coming over to do the
                 fence on Friday – have to make sure I'm in.

LORRAINE   oh that's handy

                 With a touch more than neutral appreciation...

TAYLOR'S MUM   such a nice bloke, Nick.

LORRAINE   I know.

TAYLOR'S MUM   lovely eyes

LORRAINE   he does have lovely eyes

TAYLOR'S MUM   nice hair

LORRAINE   he *does* have lovely hair.

I'm not entirely sure, but I think Sarah might have a little crush

TAYLOR'S MUM   'a little crush'?

LORRAINE *shrugs*.

ahw.

And Gethin, no ladies on the horizon?

LORRAINE   don't think so, not since whatshername, Caroline. You never know with him.

TAYLOR'S MUM   still waters run deep.

LORRAINE   not that still. He's into everything at the moment. I mean, I'm dead pleased he finished his course and everything, he's good at the film stuff, I'm sure he'll find something – more than a few shifts at the cinema

TAYLOR'S MUM   yeah that's good

LORRAINE   and there's Sarah's no interest in the schoolwork at all, but now I just wish he'd just get himself a regular job.

TAYLOR'S MUM   well.

LORRAINE   well.

TAYLOR'S MUM *flicks through the magazine*. LORRAINE *finishes up the dishes*.

TAYLOR'S MUM   Keepin' himself busy though

LORRAINE   kind of

TAYLOR'S MUM   You worried, Lorraine?

LORRAINE   no... no...

Both women want to say something, but don't.

A silence. TAYLOR'S MUM *flicks through the magazine.*

TAYLOR'S MUM *goes to speak, changes her mind.*

Beat.

TAYLOR'S MUM   You know...

LORRAINE   mm?

TAYLOR'S MUM   some of the kids – I overheard some kids outside the house. You know they sit on our wall. We hear them, with the window open. This group of girls, they were talking about Gethin, it wasn't nice

LORRAINE   really?

TAYLOR'S MUM   don't know – probably just bitching. I was surprised though, I thought they were friends of Sarah's, or in her year

LORRAINE   well, that's probably it. It probably isn't anything to do with Gethin. Girls are clever. Manipulative.

TAYLOR'S MUM   Sarah's not having problems?

LORRAINE   no no. Not any more. She's toughened up, bless her. But girls. They say things.

TAYLOR'S MUM   (*Unconvinced.*) yeah. Yeah they do.

Did they ever get the bitches that did it?

LORRAINE   not really. They all have access. They can do it on their phones and everything now. Sarah wasn't the only one. She said hers wasn't as bad as some of the others. It was obviously fake.

TAYLOR'S MUM   oh good

LORRAINE   I mean, she never showed it to me but she said
                  it was obviously like, Asian porn, an Asian
                  body with her face stuck on it

TAYLOR'S MUM   oh good

LORRAINE   I wish bullying was still as simple as when we
                  were at school. You just called someone a slut
                  and burnt their coursework.

TAYLOR'S MUM   Was it a nice Asian body?

                  LORRAINE *has finished the dishes and snorts.*

LORRAINE   I don't think so. Everything's about sex now,
                  isn't it. I mean, I never thought of myself as
                  naive, but the things you hear...

TAYLOR'S MUM   you're not naive, Lorraine

LORRAINE   ever heard 'gash'?

TAYLOR'S MUM   as in for lady bits? Yeah

LORRAINE   Ew.

TAYLOR'S MUM   Asian 'gash'.

LORRAINE   Tea or wine?

TAYLOR'S MUM   silly question

                  LORRAINE *lifts a corkscrew.*

Scene Six

TAYLOR'S MUM*'s house.*

NICK *waiting on* GETHIN. *He has the parts for the white fence, and all the tools.*

He flicks through a Daily Mail.

SARAH *passes.*

SARAH *sidles back.* NICK *glances up from his paper.*

SARAH	hi
NICK	hi
SARAH	what're you doin'?
NICK	waitin' on a bus, what's it look like?
SARAH	your mum
	Beat.
	Doin' the fence?
NICK	yep.
SARAH	hope it doesn't rain
NICK	yeah.
SARAH	see ya
NICK	bye
	SARAH *goes to leave.*
	Where's Gethin?
SARAH	sold into the sex trade far far away hopefully.
NICK	not in the house?
SARAH	unless he just isn't up yet. Possible.
NICK	I've tried his mobile

SARAH	why?
NICK	he's supposed to be here. Half an hour ago.
SARAH	God he's such a loser.
NICK	yeah.
SARAH	pity me, I'm related.
NICK	yeah.
SARAH	so are you doin' this as a favour? For Taylor's mum?
NICK	yeah
SARAH	or are you getting paid. Because she should pay you. You can't just do favours. We're in a recession.
NICK	discount
SARAH	don't be a doormat, Nick.
NICK	yeah.
	Beat.
SARAH	did you get your hair done?
NICK	what? No
SARAH	looks like highlights
NICK	what? No. Just the sun
SARAH	Well. I like it.
	Want me to help?
NICK	what?
SARAH	with the fence? Like, just till Geth gets here. I don't mind. I'm finished school today we had free periods and, like, maths, which doesn't count.
NICK	nah.
SARAH	I don't mind.

NICK   You've no idea where Geth is?

                SARAH *sighs*.

SARAH   No. I don't have, like, a sat nav, like, a Gethin
                nav, I don't, like, have a direct line to him, like
                the fucking Kremlin, what do you call it, the
                hotline from the White House –

NICK   okay.

                Beat.

                okay, you want to separate those nails? They're
                all mixed up but they should be separate, the
                shorter ones and long ones.

SARAH   okay!

                SARAH *comes over and hunches down,
                delighted.*

                We need, like, a radio

NICK   there is one.

                He puts it on.

                NICK *likes this song.*

                SARAH *hums along.*

                You know this?

SARAH   yeah, love it!

                She smiles. He smiles too.

                *She has a boogie. She's both childish, and
                womanly. So is the song. She knows most of the
                words. She gets into it.*

                GETHIN *appears suddenly.*

GETHIN   Alright, man?

                SARAH, *caught on, ducks and concentrates on
                the nail-sorting.*

NICK   Where were you?

GETHIN	sorry, sorry, I was on a roll with something, an idea, just had to get it down, you know? In the moment
NICK	we'll be in the shit if we haven't got this fence up
GETHIN	Looks like you've found yourself a slave, good work
SARAH	I was just doing the nails
GETHIN	'doing the nails?' What does that involve
SARAH	shuttup.
GETHIN	shouldn't you be at school?
SARAH	shouldn't you be… like – shouldn't you be –
GETHIN	AHHH great comeback. Excellent.

SARAH *stands up from her task, embarrassed in front of* NICK.

SARAH	I was just helping
NICK	thanks
GETHIN	have you got measles?

SARAH *looks down and covers her legs.*

What is that?

SARAH	SHAVING RASH, OKAY

SARAH *pushes past* GETHIN *and storms off.*

NICK	Mate
GETHIN	what?
NICK	she's only little
GETHIN	I didn't even do anything! She's hypersensitive.

NICK *shrugs and gets on with separating the nails.*

GETHIN *plunks himself down, idly.*

Oh my God, the *Daily Mail*? What a rag.
Fascist little rag. Did you buy this?

NICK   yeah

GETHIN   it's such a fascist / rag

NICK   do you want to do something? Like start
               marking out where the posts are going?

GETHIN   yeah yeah. Will do.

NICK   saw your Facebook Wall

GETHIN   did you? Amazing, wasn't it

NICK   How does it feel?

GETHIN   what?

NICK   to be called a perve by people who've never
               met you

GETHIN   I've blocked it now, but it took less time than I
               thought. So cool. I mean, it's scary – went right
               round and onto my Wall – haven't even been
               able to trace back how it – like who through,
               yet –

NICK   it got back to me already.

GETHIN   Who?

NICK   I'm just sayin'. I heard it before it went on
               Facebook.

GETHIN   wow. I wish Sarah'd filmed it, whatever she
               said, but then they'd know there was
               something up.

NICK   fucked up. You got Sarah to say something?

GETHIN   yep

NICK   what'd she say?

GETHIN   I don't know, do I?

NICK   what about Sarah?

GETHIN *is mildly irritated by* NICK*'s concern
for* SARAH.

GETHIN   what about Sarah? She had a great time doin'
what she does best, talking shit, should get the
public recognition she deserves

NICK   what happened to the one about all those stray
puppies getting drowned at the lough?

GETHIN   borin'

NICK   thought that was brilliant, brilliant idea for a
film

GETHIN   borin'. Low-concept, no one's interested

NICK   So now what. You've done what you wanted,
yeah. Big round of applause. You're such a
fucken weirdo, Gethin, I worry for you

GETHIN   Broomfield – some kind of Broomfield-style
exposé documentary. They love all that shit,
like when you put yourself in the shoes of the
freaks, like the guy who just ate McDonald's
for a year – did ya see that one *The Man Who
Turned into a Tree*? Channel 4 stuff. Might try
and interview that guy from that house we
filmed, Bob, do like a map of the town, how
long it took before people attacked his house.
You know he's a widower?

NICK   What if people attack your house?

GETHIN   hardly

NICK   if you're gonna go / looking for it

GETHIN   mate, A, it's not true and B, no one would
bother over some spoof from my own sister.
That's all I needed anyway, proof. So it'll stand
out from other ideas cos there's, like, evidence
in action. I'll get Sarah to be in the film. It'll be
funny, she'll be awesome. But I do still want to
interview Bob – put it up on a website maybe, a
blog, like the one we did for the football team

NICK	Leave it alone
GETHIN	what?
NICK	seriously
GETHIN	what's your problem, you're as bad as my mum
NICK	shuttup and do something, wouldya. You're supposed to be helping me
GETHIN	mate, I'm doin you a favour here
NICK	you're the one without a job – thought you needed cash
GETHIN	yeah but I've got a film-making diploma, I'm just waitin' on a break. That's what I was doing this morning, it's kind of more important you know, getting my work off the ground

A nerve. NICK's eyes flicker.

NICK	It's more important
GETHIN	yeah
NICK	Fine. Don't do me a favour, if that's how you see it. I don't need a favour. I can do the job myself.
GETHIN	She's hardly even payin' you for it anyway, you're too soft, you should charge more
NICK	look, you're pissing me off, okay? Are you gonna do the fence or not?
GETHIN	what's crawled up your arse today?
NICK	you.

Beat. Tension. Stalemate.

GETHIN	Fuck it. Sorry, mate, I can't be bothered with this.
NICK	yeah
GETHIN	don't know what side of the bed you got out of... whatever – laters

GETHIN *picks up his bag and leaves.*

NICK *carries on working.*

He turns up the radio.

Some moments.

TAYLOR'S MUM *appears with a mug of tea for him and one for herself. A smile.*

TAYLOR'S MUM   tea

NICK *turns, cloudy expression clearing, and turns down the radio again.*

He gratefully takes the tea.

NICK   cheers

TAYLOR'S MUM   Did ya want a biscuit?

NICK   nah, thanks

TAYLOR'S MUM   sure? I've Wagon Wheels

NICK   nah

TAYLOR'S MUM *fishes something out of her tea, a bit of dust.*

TAYLOR'S MUM   that Gethin there?

NICK   yeah

TAYLOR'S MUM   what'd he want?

NICK   nothin'

A moment.

TAYLOR'S MUM   Sarah?

NICK   yeah – she wanted to help

TAYLOR'S MUM   ahw.

NICK   yeah

TAYLOR'S MUM   growin' up

NICK   yeah

TAYLOR'S MUM   wearin' bras

> NICK *says nothing.*

> TAYLOR'S MUM *dunks her biscuit.*

> think she's a thing for you

NICK   nah

TAYLOR'S MUM   yeah

NICK   she's only little

TAYLOR'S MUM   (*Shrug.*) I was wild into Ziggy Stardust
before I could spell my own name

> NICK *smiles, and turns back to the fence.*

> TAYLOR'S MUM *watches him, closely.*

> You and Gethin still knock about? Friendly?

NICK   pft. Kinda

TAYLOR'S MUM   Was he gonna lend a hand...?

> Cos if you need a hand, Tom can muck in.

> *Without turning,* NICK *understands what she means.*

> I'd prefer Tom to do it.

> TAYLOR'S MUM *waits to ensure the comment lands, and wanders off.*

> NICK *turns up the radio, and stands a moment, activity suspended, biting his nails.*

Scene Seven

Night.

LORRAINE *is waiting at the dinner table. The clock ticks.*

GETHIN *breezes in.*

LORRAINE	where've you been?
GETHIN	God, it's Miss Havisham
LORRAINE	sit down
GETHIN	what's up?
LORRAINE	sit down
GETHIN	you okay, Mum?
LORRAINE	just sit there and I'll tell you

GETHIN *sits down, concerned.*

You were playing with Taylor last week?

GETHIN	what –
LORRAINE	Taylor's mum's just been over, to have a talk with me.
GETHIN	what about?
LORRAINE	she heard – she tried to tell me a few weeks ago. She heard things, about you. And when she tried to tell me she was being nice, protecting me, no one wants to hear ugly things about their...
GETHIN	This is –
LORRAINE	– no one wants that
GETHIN	– no listen, Mum – this is just –
LORRAINE	– Gethin, let me finish

GETHIN	– no because this
LORRAINE	– let me finish
GETHIN	– no / because I know
LORRAINE	SHUT UP and let me finish.
	She shrugged it off, she's a good friend. But you were playing with Taylor. Someone reported you.
GETHIN	reported me?
LORRAINE	Someone called someone. Social Services contacted Taylor's mum. Right?
GETHIN	pfff, wow
LORRAINE	and she still laughed it off.
GETHIN	yeah, should think so
LORRAINE	But they were so convincing. They were concerned, she said
(GETHIN	'concerned')
LORRAINE	which made her concerned, you see, as would any parent, I agreed, I agree with her. I agree with her. She came round here. She thought about it for a few hours and then she came round here to talk to me. She's a great friend.
GETHIN	okay – what did they say?
LORRAINE	Gethin, I don't understand what's going on, but I'm fucking sick to my stomach here. So what's going on –
GETHIN	Mum... I told you about this ages ago
LORRAINE	I really really hope you're not / going to
GETHIN	I told you what I was doing
LORRAINE	swear to God if this is what I think it is
GETHIN	and it's just a load of crap – rumours

LORRAINE	rumour?
GETHIN	yeah
LORRAINE	From where though? What started it?
GETHIN	Me! I started it – it's like, a joke – well, not a *joke* – it's a concept
LORRAINE	'concept'
GETHIN	yeah
LORRAINE	are you going to tell Social Services it's a 'concept'? Gethin? Do you think that's what you're going to say to them? Do you want to go down the street to Taylor's mother, and explain? Explain it's a 'concept'? That someone saw you with her little boy and thought something
GETHIN	Mum, I always play with Taylor – he can tell you. It's just – in a way this is exactly perfect for the project
LORRAINE	what
GETHIN	it's cool, I'll go down to Taylor's mum and tell her about it. I've it all documented and written up. You can tell her too – you know – I told you all what I was doing ages ago
LORRAINE	and I told you not to do it
GETHIN	no, you said you didn't want to hear.

Loads of people know – it's cool, it's not like a secret.

GETHIN *gets up to click the kettle.*

Tea?

Do you think she'd mind if I filmed the conversation?

LORRAINE *feels as if she's woken up on Mars.*

I mean, obviously, after I've told her what it's
about. I know it's a bit dark but it's such good
material – the industry jumps on this kinda
stuff

LORRAINE   …I… have you… ANY idea

GETHIN   Mum, don't freak out, okay? I'll nip down
tomorrow morning and explain, it'll be fine

LORRAINE   What were you doing with Taylor?

GETHIN   Mum. Playing football.

LORRAINE   Social Services, they said, the person who
reported it said you were… *holding* him –

GETHIN   what d'you mean?

LORRAINE   just tell me – you played football and what
else?

GETHIN   Mum, it's football

LORRAINE   he's seven. Christ, did you touch / him?

GETHIN   Jesus, what do / you mean?

LORRAINE   – of course not that I mean at all – I mean in
the way that you're not supposed to go near
other people's kids in this day and age in any
way that could be misconstrued, I mean did
you touch him physically I mean how could it
have been misconstrued?

GETHIN   You can ask Taylor himself. We kick the ball
around and he loves it when you play-wrestle
him to the ground to get the ball off him.
We've done it loads of times – it's messing
about –

LORRAINE   'messing about'

GETHIN   yeah

LORRAINE   well, you get down there tonight, and you clear
up 'messing about' to his mother, okay?
Because she's not so sure. She's scared.

GETHIN   so ridiculous

                LORRAINE*'s knuckles are white.*

LORRAINE   you're lucky she hasn't told Tom. She was
                scared and I could see it. Okay? I could tell.
                And she came here, because she's a good
                friend. And you, you are never, ever to go back
                to this 'project'

GETHIN   look, sorry, Mum, but you don't understand
                it –

LORRAINE   No

GETHIN   it's an idea about difficult issues

LORRAINE   No more

GETHIN   you can't tell me what to do

LORRAINE   If you live under this roof

GETHIN   God, Mum

LORRAINE   Do you hear me?

                Do you HEAR ME?

GETHIN   YES. God. I said I'll go down, okay? There's
                no point in trying to speak sense to you till
                you've chilled out. This is exactly my point –

                LORRAINE, *upset, leaves the room with*
                GETHIN *still talking.*

                GETHIN *shakes his head. Pours his cup of tea*
                and puts in his headphones.

Scene Eight

SARAH, *on a street corner trying to smoke, in her school uniform.*

NICK, *heading out for the evening, in a fresh shirt.*

He nods to SARAH.

SARAH *makes a show of turning away, taking a drag on her cigarette, but she overdoes it, tries to stifle a coughing fit, tears in her eyes.*

NICK	alright?
SARAH	fine.
NICK	shouldn't smoke
SARAH	thanks, Mum
	NICK *sees her face, slows, hesitates.*
NICK	cryin'?
SARAH	NO
NICK	since when did you smoke
SARAH	it, like, calms my nerves
	NICK *hovers, uncertain.*
	Goin' out?
NICK	yeah. Pub.
SARAH	someone special?
NICK	no
	Beat.
	SARAH *goes for another drag, splutters, thinks better of it, and huffs.*
	NICK *moves off a few steps.*

	Gethin'll kill ya if he sees ya with that
SARAH	Gethin can KISS my ARSE
	NICK *slows again.*
	What?
NICK	just…
	you okay?
SARAH	do I look okay?
NICK	what's wrong
SARAH	bitches in school. I'm gonna napalm them all to death
NICK	givin' you a hard time?
SARAH	All I said was – ugGH – whatever.
NICK	but you're okay
	SARAH *stares at him.*
SARAH	yeah. I'm BRILLIANT.
	Is that Cool Water?
	SARAH *steps towards him.*
NICK	What. Me?
SARAH	yeah
NICK	yeah
SARAH	smells amazin'
NICK	I like it.
SARAH	I love it
NICK	well… see ya
SARAH	uh – Nick
	SARAH *steps closer.*
	Thanks for askin'
NICK	s'okay

SARAH   people never ask

                        SARAH, *possessed by a will she doesn't quite*
                        herself understand, stumbles into NICK *in a*
                        clumsy attempt to kiss him.

                        NICK *blocks her, holds her firmly at arm's*
                        length, looks at her, surprised.

NICK   what're you doing?

SARAH   READIN' A BOOK

NICK   look –

SARAH   get off me, don't TOUCH me

                        Her words shock NICK.

NICK   I'm not touchin' you!

SARAH   God, I know you're desperate –

NICK   Get away from me

                        His vehemence shocks SARAH.

SARAH   what?

NICK   just... go home

                        (*To himself.*) ... like, you're like twelve

                        NICK *shakes his head and continues on his*
                        way, only looking back once.

SARAH   (*Flustered, shouts.*) want a photo?

                        (*Quieter.*) Freak.

                        When he has gone, she self-consciously stamps
                        out the cigarette, spits out the disgusting taste,
                        pulls her jacket closer and shuffles off,
                        coughing.

Scene Nine

LAYLA *sits in a police office plastic chair.*

LAYLA   sorry, yeah.

Uhh. It's something – it's something I never. I never did nothing about it then – at the time – cos I – you know I was embarrassed. Stupid. Stupid to have… But then I didn't think. I didn't know. He was – I went out with him for like, seven months, which is like for ever when you're like sixteen. And he was older so it was really, like, cool. He had a Corsa. He was really nice. I don't really – I don't think he would've meant to… he was – I donno – must've been twenty-one? Twenty. Four years older. Well, three and a half. But he was so sweet, he never made me feel little, you know? You know what, he didn't even sleep with me. Swear to God. Even though we went out for so long, isn't that cool? Amazing? In this day and age. I mean, we lied, we said we'd done it cos otherwise his friends would've been assholes. Mine too. But we never did. Well, we did eventually, like after we broke up, like. Anyway. Kind of. Chivalrous or something. But the phones with cameras, everyone has them now. They've got like super-cameras like underwater optical-zoom fifty-megapixel shit and stuff – sorry – I've a really nice Nokia – but those were only out really, the good ones, when we were going out. Nick had one. We were messing about, just. You know. And it was really hot. Really hot I think, he had his T-shirt off first. We were, you know. Messing about. And I took

my top off, it was a top from H&M, ~~nice~~
~~maroon vest so it was~~. I took it off you know
and my bra – I mean it is, it was half my fault
– and he took this stupid fucking picture – and
I was like 'delete it! Gross! I look like an
ALIEN or something!' But he was like 'no,
it's beautiful.' He said – I know I'm a muppet
– but at the time it was so like – he said it
would be like in olden times when they carried
little portraits and sexy pictures of their muses
or something – seriously don't know where he
came up with that stuff – so he didn't delete it.
Like, I don't know, I seriously don't know
how it came to be… I mean, all I know is that
the only other person who had such a snazzy
phone, or who would've had like, access to
Nick's or who – and I can't believe he would –
but if Nick *did* show him – he swears to God
he didn't – but I mean, I was out of school for
like two months. I had to repeat after the
summer. And starting a new school in
September was like, the most mortifying,
humiliating thing I've ever had to do. ~~Some of~~
~~the teachers knew, but they didn't really know~~
~~how to deal with it I think. It wasn't in the~~
~~papers or anything the way it is now~~ – they
~~had other problems you know?~~ And I didn't
want any action taken – I just wanted to like,
disappear. It felt like – like –

I just wanted it to disappear.

Or for me to disappear.

I don't know.

God. I – it felt so… *uhhgh*.

I tried to disappear – if you know what I
mean…

LAYLA *pulls down her sleeves. She
disappears for a moment.*

... everything felt so shit. But. He did that. I know it was him. He was always so pervy – he always carried this fucking video camera around with him. I don't know. So when someone said – the other day someone said about how they'd heard he was – you know, like – bent or something. I thought. I don't want anyone else to go through that. I told my mum. She said I should come here. Not for me. Not so much. But in case there're others. In case it wasn't a one-off, you know? I don't want to waste anyone's time. I just thought. You know? I should. You know? Say.

Scene Ten

The police station.

GETHIN *sits, confident but alert, face-on.*

AUTHORITY	Have you ever filmed children?
GETHIN	No
AUTHORITY	Come on, surely you have.
GETHIN	No
AUTHORITY	Don't lie.
GETHIN	I'm not lying
AUTHORITY	You have a video camera, chances are you'll have captured kids on there
GETHIN	Incidentally, maybe, yeah
AUTHORITY	Incidentally.
GETHIN	Well, for cutaway
AUTHORITY	Cutaway?
GETHIN	Cutaway material, background stuff.

AUTHORITY   You'd have filmed kids for 'cutaway material' then.

GETHIN   Yeah. It's a film term.

AUTHORITY   So for example

GETHIN   You can't just film anyone, you have to sign release forms and all that bureaucratic stuff. Only an idiot would film kids.

AUTHORITY   What age?

GETHIN   I don't know, kids

AUTHORITY   Young?

GETHIN   Yes young, definition of kids

AUTHORITY   You've probably incidentally filmed kids for background material

GETHIN   ...yeah.

AUTHORITY   How did it feel?

GETHIN   What do you mean?

AUTHORITY   How did it feel to film them –

    A bit more twitchy.

GETHIN   What kind of questions are these? You're trying to make out that –

AUTHORITY   Please just answer the questions. No one's out to get you.

GETHIN   I don't know – no – they're leading questions – and I've already explained to you. It's all under control.

    Can you request the transcript of these interviews afterwards?

AUTHORITY   This interview? What for?

GETHIN   So I can include it. In the project.

AUTHORITY   The project – tell us again? The idea...

GETHIN	It's all on my computer. Everyone knows. I told people about it. It's all documented. It's research. Just ask Mum and Sarah and my mate, my mate Nick.
AUTHORITY	We are. We have.
GETHIN	Good.
AUTHORITY	You're a very confident young man.
GETHIN	Well...
AUTHORITY	It comes across as inappropriate. Given the serious nature of what we're discussing. Can you see how that would be the case?
GETHIN	Well, I can't explain it any more clearly. You won't find anything inappropriate about me. It's, like, if you'd just listen to me, everything that's happened and what you've said exactly proves the point I've been trying to make. It's ironic. You've already decided I'm whatever and you're treating me like that, but once you realise that's *part* of the whole thing
AUTHORITY	You're not making sense to us, Gethin
GETHIN	like – you research, right? For this job?
AUTHORITY	I'm not sure that's a good comparison
GETHIN	Look, then ask Sarah. She knows where the miniDVs are, I've already offered to get them. I'll get them for you – I've been recording it all, the process. And it's on my laptop.
AUTHORITY	We've looked
GETHIN	What?
	GETHIN *stiffens*.
AUTHORITY	On your computer
GETHIN	you've looked?
AUTHORITY	There are a lot of pictures of yourself on there.

GETHIN	You've already got it? From home? Okay… ahm then you'll know / I'm just
AUTHORITY	There's some of you naked. Images. What are they for?
GETHIN	God

GETHIN *laughs incredulously, glances away.*

He picks up the empty plastic cup, looks in it, sets it down.

AUTHORITY	What are they for?
GETHIN	I don't know
AUTHORITY	You don't know.
GETHIN	they're just…
AUTHORITY	Why do you take pictures of yourself naked?
GETHIN	they're old. They're just… I was you know, workin' out, I wanted to… measure my progress
AUTHORITY	When did you take them?
GETHIN	I don't know, when I came out of the shower?
AUTHORITY	When, as in dates
GETHIN	(*Shaking his head.*) I don't know, a year, two years ago?
AUTHORITY	Did you want to distribute them?
GETHIN	distribute / them?
AUTHORITY	Distribute them
GETHIN	No – they're just – I just… I… it's just like I was curious
AUTHORITY	You've never shown them to anyone
GETHIN	no way, it's just me, just *my* photos of me
AUTHORITY	Of course they're your photos, we just want you to explain them

GETHIN   They're private

AUTHORITY   Sorry, but for the moment, 'private' is exactly what we need to talk about.

GETHIN   They're just pictures for me, though, of me, it's hardly illegal

AUTHORITY   Do you mean, they're self-/portraits?

GETHIN   – yeah… I mean… I don't know what I mean

AUTHORITY   You don't know?

GETHIN   I didn't think about it that deeply – it's my computer in my room, not going anywhere, they could be nudes for like, photography, like art

AUTHORITY   You would say they were art?

GETHIN   no, not these, particular – it's *embarrassing* – but I'm sure I'm not the only one who ever – I mean, I'm just comparing, you can't have a go at me for having pictures of myself, that belong to me

AUTHORITY   How does it make you feel to look at those images

GETHIN   of myself?

AUTHORITY   Yes

GETHIN   nothing. I see myself every day, it's no great shakes

AUTHORITY   Your genitalia

GETHIN   well, yeah I do recognise it from when I take a leak

AUTHORITY   …

GETHIN   'genitalia'… pft

AUTHORITY   But you download images from the internet too, don't you

GETHIN   yeah, everyone does

AUTHORITY   There're pictures from the internet on there, that don't belong to you

GETHIN   Maybe some, yeah. That's what the internet's for, resources – including images. Obviously. That's what the internet's for.

AUTHORITY   Not all images

GETHIN   seriously, it's like the main resource for information, common sharing, images are totally up for grabs as long as you credit the copyright. You're not gonna do me for breach of copyright? People do it all the time. / Is that what this is?

AUTHORITY   They do. Still breaking the law.

GETHIN   most kids do their research on there now, and businesses, all their photos and images

AUTHORITY   It's not so straightforward

GETHIN   Come on, it's not the nineties. It's weird – you know – the authorities are still full of technology illiterate people – who're afraid of what they don't get – like, everyone across the country probably has stuff that's technically breach of copyright

AUTHORITY   What's 'MEINENSCHAFT'

GETHIN   …

AUTHORITY   Gethin?

GETHIN   A folder

AUTHORITY   Yes

GETHIN   my folder on there

AUTHORITY   Yes

GETHIN   It's just porn. Jesus.

AUTHORITY   What's 'Meinenschaft' mean?

GETHIN   It's German

AUTHORITY   Yes

GETHIN   I made it up – 'My craft' like, my work. It's like, I don't know

AUTHORITY   What?

GETHIN   I made it when I was like fourteen, learning German, in case Mum was on there – she wouldn't notice it. I wasn't going to label it PORN, was I?

AUTHORITY   Fourteen?

GETHIN   It's just porn

AUTHORITY   A lot of it

GETHIN   Really? Ten years is a long time to collect a lot of anything. It's normal. You know? Every boy has it, don't try and say, it's not like you can insinuate

AUTHORITY   Do they?

GETHIN   YES, come on

AUTHORITY   Why didn't you want anyone to know?

GETHIN   Oh my God are you serious?

AUTHORITY   What kind of pornography do you like most?

GETHIN   To be honest I don't bother much any more

AUTHORITY   Do you have any other pictures, of people you know? Your sister for example?

GETHIN   What?

AUTHORITY   Your sister

GETHIN   don't talk about her like that

AUTHORITY   Do you masturbate?

GETHIN   Shut up!

AUTHORITY   Why? It's just a question. Surely it's normal. Every boy masturbates. Girls do too.

GETHIN   No – I didn't – to pictures, no

AUTHORITY	Okay.
GETHIN	Oh my God. No.
AUTHORITY	We're just trying to establish the degree / of
GETHIN	'Degree of' what?
AUTHORITY	Settle down.
GETHIN	Don't – I am settled. Because this is ridiculous. This is ridiculous. 'The degree of' – I wish I was filming this.
AUTHORITY	Do you?
GETHIN	Yeah.
AUTHORITY	Why?
GETHIN	To show – to show how ridiculous this is
AUTHORITY	You think this is ridiculous
GETHIN	Yes
AUTHORITY	You think, you're not ridiculous but everyone else is
GETHIN	At this point in time
AUTHORITY	Is that why you think you can film them?
GETHIN	What? What are you, what do / you mean –
AUTHORITY	You've expressed that feeling a few times already. It sounds a bit like, I don't know, delusions of grandeur. Do you know what we mean by that?
GETHIN	I know what you mean
AUTHORITY	Have you ever been diagnosed as bipolar? Do you know what that is? Have you often had delusions of grandeur?
	Have you ever had thoughts about doing things you know are impossible? Or things you shouldn't do?
GETHIN	No I'm not –

AUTHORITY	But you've been treated for depression?
GETHIN	…
AUTHORITY	You went to counselling
GETHIN	Yeah, when Dad left, so?
AUTHORITY	You've suffered depression
GETHIN	Uhm, surprise. Dad leaves, kid depressed.
AUTHORITY	Your dad left
GETHIN	yep
AUTHORITY	How did that make you feel?
GETHIN	well obviously, you've already answered that. They made me see a teacher, the counsellor.
AUTHORITY	Do you see your dad?
GETHIN	No. Not really.
AUTHORITY	Why?
GETHIN	what's it got to do with anything? cos he's a knob and he left us. And he's thick and hardly worked a day in his life and he ties his trainers really tight.
AUTHORITY	You're angry?
GETHIN	I'm over it
AUTHORITY	Do you struggle with these feelings?
GETHIN	no.
AUTHORITY	Your dad left –
GETHIN	so we've established –
AUTHORITY	But his brother still lived on your street, for a few years, didn't he?
GETHIN	yeah.
AUTHORITY	That must've been hard. When he didn't visit you. But your uncle still lived there. Rory.

GETHIN   what's it got to do with anything.

AUTHORITY   Just building a picture

GETHIN   I'm over it. Rory was cool.

AUTHORITY   Are you still in touch with him?

GETHIN   no. He moved away too when I was like, a kid.

AUTHORITY   What was cool about him?

GETHIN   pft you're weird. I don't know. He had a cool
              motorbike? (*Dismissive*.) I was a kid. He had a
              motorbike.

AUTHORITY   Did he like you?

GETHIN   probably annoyed the hell out of him.

AUTHORITY   What made you think that?

GETHIN   just. Probably did.

AUTHORITY   So you liked him

GETHIN   he was okay

AUTHORITY   Still in touch with him?

GETHIN   (I told you) he moved away

AUTHORITY   Do you ever want to hurt yourself?

GETHIN   GOD.

AUTHORITY   Did you?

GETHIN   What do you want me to say? I sat alone
              listening to Marilyn Manson backwards? I was
              fine. I played football.

AUTHORITY   Can you explain your search history? On your
              computer. It doesn't read very pleasantly

GETHIN   RESEARCH. The websites and stuff, it's all
              research, obviously – you guys, you have to
              research things don't you, to do this job?

AUTHORITY   As a team. Under supervision.

GETHIN	well…
AUTHORITY	What?
GETHIN	it's like what I was saying earlier, someone has to do it. If no one did anything because of fear there'd be no, like, thinking. I mean, that's like America all over, it's all self-censorship.
AUTHORITY	What are you talking about?
GETHIN	I'm saying it's like in China where they have restricted internet access and everything, they don't want people to think.
AUTHORITY	And you do. Think.
GETHIN	yeah, that's what I'm trying to do
AUTHORITY	So what did you 'think' you were doing?
GETHIN	don't say it like that
AUTHORITY	Like what? What you're telling me is that you saw yourself, you imagined fame and success. You fantasised that your 'research' would be made into a groundbreaking film.
GETHIN	I didn't say it like that
AUTHORITY	Sorry. How did you say it?
GETHIN	Can we take a break?
AUTHORITY	…
GETHIN	please. I need to… I need to piss
AUTHORITY	Okay.
GETHIN	just so you know I'll probably see my own penis. Is that okay?
AUTHORITY	Do you think sarcasm is appropriate?
GETHIN	sorry, I'm not trying to be, I'm just trying to make the point
AUTHORITY	You'll have time.

Elsewhere, SARAH, *looking small and dishevelled, beside* LORRAINE, *who is pacing.*

LORRAINE   stupid stupid arrogant

SARAH   Mum

LORRAINE   spoilt

SARAH   MUM

LORRAINE   you two have had everything. You haven't struggled. I don't know why you would do this.

SARAH   it was, like, a joke

LORRAINE   you think you're funnier than abuse? Cleverer than the police?

SARAH   well, I didn't know everyone was gonna go crazy

LORRAINE   do you know what, we're cursed. We're friggin' cursed, this family

SARAH   what're you talking about

LORRAINE   no idea, either of you. Stupid children.

SARAH   like, hello, I'm sixteen

LORRAINE   like, hello, you're a stupid stupid child

SARAH   *Mum*

LORRAINE   you I can almost forgive for being stupid, but him. It's my own fault. You've had this smooth, spoilt little life. I don't know. I don't know

SARAH   Mum, you're freaking me out

             LORRAINE *leans intently into* SARAH's *moody face.*

LORRAINE   freaking *you* out? After everything we got through, after everything, this. I worked my

arse off to give youse everything you bloody
needed. To get through it – I knew I knew
there'd be no end to it, this sickness…

LORRAINE *wipes away a silent tear.*

AUTHORITY   Could you wait outside, Lorraine?

LORRAINE *shakes her head.*

LORRAINE *leaves.*

SARAH *huffs.*

Sarah, can you describe for me your
relationship with your brother?

SARAH   He's annoying

AUTHORITY   What do you mean?

SARAH   Well, he's a big brother, isn't he

AUTHORITY   How does he annoy you?

SARAH   Just by existing, normally

AUTHORITY   Have you ever talked to anyone about this?

SARAH   No. I mean it's normal. I mean, God, he's not
that bad.

AUTHORITY   But you just told us you found him annoying.

SARAH   Yeah but like…

AUTHORITY   Do you miss your dad?

SARAH   not really.

AUTHORITY   Why?

SARAH   cos he's a total knobhead losertron.

AUTHORITY   Do you like school?

SARAH   not bothered, why?

AUTHORITY   Does Gethin ever talk about your dad?

SARAH   without using the words 'dick' and 'head'? No.

AUTHORITY   Has Gethin ever been physical with you?

SARAH   Weird. What do you mean?

AUTHORITY   Sarah, we were told that you confided in a
             schoolmate recently. About the nature of your
             brother's behaviour

SARAH   Oh... I said some stupid stuff

AUTHORITY   What stuff?

SARAH   I said a load of rubbish. It was like a bet. Set
             up. I already told someone all this, I already
             spoke to someone

AUTHORITY   But why would you say something that wasn't
             true?

SARAH   I don't know

AUTHORITY   You were lying?

SARAH   people lie all the time and stuff

AUTHORITY   But people don't normally lie about things like
             that

SARAH   I know. Okay. I'm sorry okay. I'm sorry for
             stuff.

AUTHORITY   You don't need to apologise, Sarah.

             You know, you can tell us anything. You don't
             need to be afraid

             Beat. SARAH *fronts it out.*

SARAH   I'm not afraid – I don't need to say anything

             Beat.

AUTHORITY   Do you like art?

SARAH   like, Hitler was an artist

AUTHORITY   ...

SARAH   enough said.

AUTHORITY   Tell us about when you fainted in art class.

             SARAH *perks up slightly.*

SARAH	OhmyGod I just passed out it was weird
AUTHORITY	Were you frightened?
SARAH	no. It was funny
AUTHORITY	And then you went home.
SARAH	yeah. To recover. Recuperate.
AUTHORITY	Because your school aren't sure you fainted.
SARAH	what?
AUTHORITY	They're concerned that you didn't actually pass out. That you faked it. To get out of class.
SARAH	no way, I was totally out of it, I totally passed out. Probably low blood sugar or something, I just needed a Kit Kat Chunky, I'm probably hypoglycaemic
AUTHORITY	Your art teacher wasn't certain either
SARAH	she's such a dried-up munt that one – Old Bat in the Cave
AUTHORITY	'Bat in the cave'?
SARAH	bogeys. She always has a bat in the cave.
AUTHORITY	She told us she's very fond of you. SARAH *squirms the slightest bit.* She thinks that art class is hard for you. You're in with the same group, those girls. The ones who upset you earlier this year –
SARAH	Oh my God get over it. *Silence.* When can I go?
AUTHORITY	Are those the girls you told about Gethin?
SARAH	not really. Some of them maybe.
AUTHORITY	How did it feel to get their attention?

SARAH   I don't even care.

AUTHORITY   Like when you pretended to faint. Did it feel
             good?

SARAH   I can't believe you. You can't just go around
             callin' people a liar. I could actually probably
             sue you and stuff, yeah for libel

AUTHORITY   You look afraid.

SARAH   I'm afraid of you, making me say things

AUTHORITY   No one's making you say things. Do you feel
             like you've been made to say things before?

SARAH   Maybe

AUTHORITY   By Gethin?

SARAH   No! That / was just messin' around –

AUTHORITY   He asked you to say things and you talked to
             those girls, the ones who circulated a
             pornographic image with your face on it, didn't
             they?

SARAH   but that was like, that was like whatever, God
             you're like obsessed.

AUTHORITY   It's okay, Sarah.

             SARAH *is getting agitated.*

             She pulls her sleeves down over her hands,
             plucking at them.

SARAH   this is so frustrating.

AUTHORITY   Take your time. Take your time.

             Sarah, have you ever heard of Layla Fields?

SARAH   Yeah.

             Why?

AUTHORITY   What does the name mean to you?

SARAH   She was this girl a few years above

AUTHORITY	Is that all?
SARAH	She went out with someone – used to hang around our street, for a while
AUTHORITY	What else?
SARAH	I don't know
AUTHORITY	Anything else about Layla?
SARAH	I don't know – she was pretty, not a total munt. She was small. She used to always be in the passenger seat of Nick's Corsa.
AUTHORITY	Nick?
SARAH	They were going out. Nick's Gethin's best mate. They're mates.
AUTHORITY	Nick's girlfriend Layla. That's right. And did Gethin like her too?
SARAH	I don't know. Weird.
AUTHORITY	Do you think he did?
SARAH	I don't know. Probably.
	She broke up with Nick but Gethin said he could do better anyway, she was like frigid.
AUTHORITY	Why did he say that?
SARAH	Cos she was probably.
AUTHORITY	Their relationship wasn't good?
SARAH	They kissed like all the time, puke, but I know Layla's little sister and she's frigid too. She gets called Electrolux at school. You know Electrolux? They make fridges. It's cos their dad's a big Bible-basher. The worst thing ever was when this topless photo of Layla went round school and she like had a breakdown and disappeared for a term. That was weird.
AUTHORITY	Did you see it?

SARAH	What? The photo?
AUTHORITY	Yes.
SARAH	Yeah it was hilarious
AUTHORITY	You did –
SARAH	– it was so embarrassing – everyone saw it – she's like half in the dark but it's totally her, in a car, and she's smiling, like this big massive smile and she just totally has no top on, it's so weird and awful
AUTHORITY	You saw it on a phone.
SARAH	Yeah, Gethin's
AUTHORITY	You saw it on Gethin's phone.
SARAH	Yeah it went round everybody
AUTHORITY	Had everyone already seen it then?
SARAH	can't remember. Don't think it was till later cos she was off school like after the summer holidays and that was like a while after everyone had seen it
AUTHORITY	So you saw it before it went round properly, on Gethin's phone.

The colour drains from SARAH*'s face.*

SARAH	…can't remember
AUTHORITY	Gethin showed you it. Where did he get it?
SARAH	Can't remember.
AUTHORITY	What age were you, Sarah?
SARAH	Dunno
AUTHORITY	You were thirteen. You'd have been thirteen
SARAH	Suppose
AUTHORITY	Why would your older brother show you an image like that?

SARAH   It wasn't like that – it – it was just funny – it
               was blurry – and she was so whiney – it was
               just like a funny thing

AUTHORITY   Not funny for Layla

SARAH   Obviously.

AUTHORITY   Why are you crying, Sarah

SARAH   Because you've made it out like, you've
               twisted this whole thing

AUTHORITY   We haven't said anything, Sarah. If you've told
               us the truth, then we haven't done anything to
               upset you. So why are you really upset?

               What did you confide in your friends at school?

SARAH   Nothing!

AUTHORITY   Why aren't you telling us the truth now?

SARAH   Please, please let me talk to Gethin.

AUTHORITY   We don't think that's a good idea.

SARAH   please

AUTHORITY   You know how Layla Fields felt. Don't you.
               You know how that feels. Those girls made
               you feel like that.

SARAH   I don't like this

AUTHORITY   It's okay, Sarah.

               Do you remember Rory?

SARAH   can I see Mum?

AUTHORITY   Just a few more questions

SARAH   No I don't remember Rory I was in a fucking
               pram probably. Can I see my mum now?

               NICK *and* LORRAINE *sit in a waiting area.*

               *There are three uncomfortable seats. They sit
               with an empty seat between them.*

LORRAINE sniffs, eyes vacant, lost in thought.

NICK sits still, arms crossed, leg jiggling slightly.

LORRAINE turns to say something to NICK, but can't bring herself to.

She stands, unsteady, to leave.

NICK doesn't look up, his expression is thoughtful.

NICK   Fuck you, Lorraine.

LORRAINE catches her breath, falls apart within herself.

She walks carefully away from him.

SARAH is escorted past.

NICK looks up, relieved.

are you okay? – Is she okay?

SARAH   God

NICK   what'd they say?

SARAH   help him will ya? – Please

NICK   but you're okay?

SARAH   YEAH but Nick it's all a loada shit

NICK   right

SARAH   it's all wrong

NICK   I know

SARAH   They're getting it all wrong

NICK   Sarah...

sure?

SARAH looks at him like he's crazy.

SARAH   YES

NICK searches for the truth in her face.

NICK	yeah
SARAH	it's a loada shit you *know* it is
NICK	I know
SARAH	why're they all such dicks?
	SARAH*'s face crumples: she hides it from him.*
	NICK *sees it. Her clarity. And nods, satisfied.*
NICK	okay
	Don't worry
	Okay?
	Elsewhere, GETHIN, *increasingly agitated.*
GETHIN	What do you mean there aren't any files?
AUTHORITY	There aren't any files.
GETHIN	You're lying.
AUTHORITY	Lying?
GETHIN	yeah
AUTHORITY	There are no files matching your description.
GETHIN	no, they're all on there
AUTHORITY	Tell us about your movie collection
GETHIN	it's all on there COME ON
AUTHORITY	Tell us about your taste in movies.
GETHIN	Where's Nick? Did you call him?
AUTHORITY	Quite an eclectic range.
GETHIN	Where's my mum, she'll tell you
AUTHORITY	Were they on the syllabus, for your course?
GETHIN	where's my mum
AUTHORITY	She's at home. She's upset.
GETHIN	she's gone home?

AUTHORITY	Yes.
GETHIN	home?
AUTHORITY	Yes.
GETHIN	does she know I'm still here?
AUTHORITY	Yes.

Beat.

GETHIN	Where's Sarah?
AUTHORITY	She's working with other members of our team.
GETHIN	Look.

GETHIN *is sweating, panicking.*

AUTHORITY	...
GETHIN	Look, I've been responsible. You have to have responsibility, I get it. The difference is this was all fake, a performance, not real.
AUTHORITY	So, you would say you've been doing a performance. For who?
GETHIN	It's all explained. I had a pre-production schedule. It was all planned out.
AUTHORITY	What did Sarah tell her peers?
GETHIN	I don't know
AUTHORITY	You / don't know.
GETHIN	I don't know the details
AUTHORITY	You don't. Exactly. That doesn't sound planned. Or responsible. That sounds convenient. Unlikely.
GETHIN	it was spur-of-the-moment
AUTHORITY	So it wasn't planned.
GETHIN	no – yes, but / no

AUTHORITY   You sound confused. Do you feel confused?
              It's often unplanned to touch another person
              inappropriately. Perhaps you wouldn't plan to
              touch your sister.

              Terror explodes across GETHIN*'s face.*

GETHIN   Call Nick – he can recover / the files

AUTHORITY   It's best for us all if you / answer our
              questions.

GETHIN   and he knows too – he knows. Call Nick. Call
              Nick.

              Please.

AUTHORITY   We already have.

GETHIN   And?

              Is he here?

AUTHORITY   And is he the only other person you claim
              knows about your alleged 'project'?

GETHIN   yeah he knows about it, totally – he was with
              me, he'll tell you, it was never like a secret. I
              started a blog about it.

AUTHORITY   So did the kids who did those school shootings
              in the States.

GETHIN   Ask Nick. Ask him.

AUTHORITY   Mm.

GETHIN   'Mm' what?

              sorry, 'mm' what?

              What?

Scene Eleven

GETHIN *sits, head low, biting his nails.*

NICK *sits stony, opposite.*

Elsewhere, TAYLOR'S MUM *has a cold cup of tea and waits for her friend to call, mobile laid in front of her.*

SARAH *rubs away a silent tear, digs out her cigarettes, but can't stomach lighting one.*

LORRAINE *sits, hands clasped under her chin, glassy-eyed, torn apart, timeless.*

LAYLA *tries on a new top in the mirror. She doesn't much like what she sees.*

AUTHORITY *completes paperwork.*

LORRAINE   Say sorry

TAYLOR'S MUM   feel sick

SARAH   love you

LAYLA   is it true?

AUTHORITY   You know.

GETHIN   Where's / the...

NICK   this is fun.

GETHIN   Nick, seriously

NICK   yeah

GETHIN   I just need you to recover some files from my laptop

                Beat.

NICK   yeah?

GETHIN   What's wrong with you? This is fucking serious

NICK	I know.
	I know it's serious. I think I cottoned on to that before you
GETHIN	so what's with the attitude
NICK	what'd you expect?
GETHIN	I didn't – well, obviously I didn't think it'd go insane – I didn't anticipate everyone being stupid
NICK	who's stupid?
GETHIN	– what – I'm sorry about the fence okay? Whatever it is
(NICK	'the fence')
GETHIN	whatever it is that's up with you, I think this is a bit more important – I mean we're mates so
NICK	yep.
	Mates.
GETHIN	so. Would you talk to them?
NICK	depends. What do you want me to say?
GETHIN	the truth obviously – I don't *want* you to say anything, just the facts. Just the like, facts.
NICK	okay.
	Okay.
	I'll have to tell them there aren't any documents on your computer supporting what you say.
GETHIN	what?
NICK	that'll be awkward
	GETHIN, *rigid*.
	Elsewhere in the world, everybody shifts slightly.
GETHIN	how come?

NICK	can't believe we're sitting here
GETHIN	how come?
NICK	I wiped them.
GETHIN	What. The. Fuck. Are you joking?
NICK	no
GETHIN	off – off my laptop?
NICK	yep
GETHIN	are you messing, mate?
NICK	no
GETHIN	what the – what the fucking FUCK is wrong with you?
NICK	wrong with *me*?
	Wrong with me?
GETHIN	look, what is going ON. I need you to tell them. What're you doing?
NICK	what're *you* doing?
GETHIN	Mum's gone weird and Sarah – they're fucking with people's heads, and that's all fine as long as I am evidently – as long as there is evidence that this is all – you know – all a misunderstanding. I can't believe Mum's gone home
NICK	Lorraine's really upset
GETHIN	(*Angry.*) God, she's ridiculous
NICK	she's upset
GETHIN	how could she be so stupid
NICK	never you, is it
GETHIN	*what?* I'm INNOCENT – Nick, I haven't done anything wrong, you know me. I shouldn't even be here. This is a joke. This is completely crazy

NICK	I never saw anyone else laughing. You just assumed everyone was in on your weird little plan
GETHIN	it wasn't a 'little plan' – I'm not out to – I was never out to hurt anyone – this has all completely blown up, but you guys, I mean the whole point is that it was all planned and you guys were in on it –
NICK	No. No, we weren't
GETHIN	but this is different, this isn't, this isn't the way it was meant to happen and now you're fucking me over – what the fuck?
NICK	you're either really really stupid, or really really clever – all the shit about artistic freedom – and you're always saying stuff just to provoke everyone you know you're always saying shit but all this
GETHIN	No one's listening to me
NICK	Wasn't that the intention? The plan? That was your plan though – sounds like a success –
GETHIN	why's no one listening
NICK	or a double bluff, to me. It could be a double bluff.
GETHIN	double bluff?
NICK	Are you surprised people aren't rushing to defend you?
GETHIN	I don't get it, mate. Why're you doing this? Why're you – you know me
NICK	Do I? Christ, Gethin, I don't know. I don't know if I do know the person who'd pull such a sick fucking stunt
GETHIN	what's sick? I didn't do anything
NICK	You DID. You ARE. Why do you keep lying?

A breath.

GETHIN *stares at* NICK, *who is trembling.*

GETHIN   what is it?

                What do you mean?

                Beat.

LAYLA   Say sorry

SARAH   feel sick

LORRAINE   love you

TAYLOR'S MUM   say sorry

GETHIN   I don't know what you mean

NICK   It's funny, do you know what was brought up?
                That picture of Layla.

                Beat.

                Did they mention that to you?

GETHIN   what?

                No.

LAYLA   Sorry

AUTHORITY   sick

NICK   They must be gathering evidence. Building a
                profile. You are so fucked, mate.

SARAH /   is that true?
LAYLA

GETHIN   Layla Fields

NICK   yep. You know I know it was you, don't you

GETHIN   …

NICK   I know it was

GETHIN   uh, / I don't –

NICK	don't you dare fucking lie – you were the only one I showed it to
SARAH	say sorry
GETHIN	that was, ah fuck. I didn't mean to... I...
NICK	sent it around, started it off
GETHIN	I literally only sent it to Jonty – honest to God – I didn't think he'd know who it was
TAYLOR'S MUM	true?
NICK	you sick cunt
GETHIN	is that what this is about? Cos that's messed up, Nick
NICK	messed up
GETHIN	it was only tits it wasn't even you know –
NICK	'minge'?
GETHIN	mate
NICK	That was my girlfriend.
GETHIN	okay sorry, okay?
NICK	she had to repeat
GETHIN	sorry
NICK	you're not though. You weren't
GETHIN	why are they bringing that up now? That was ages ago
NICK	you know
GETHIN	that was an accident
AUTHORITY / LORRAINE	Is it true?
SARAH	say sorry
NICK	You could be like him. How can I tell? How can anyone tell?

GETHIN	Nick, what're you talking about
NICK	I just can't tell with you. Cos I think I know you. But now this. This can of worms it just makes you think. Makes you stop and think like, because you'd never usually stop and think like that
GETHIN	I don't know what you're saying
NICK	and you just kept going on and on – at first I just thought it was like some weird sick-fuck joke, you were just getting your kicks out of it, getting at me for something and maybe it *was* nothing – I don't even know – but then. I started to think. Why would anyone do that? Mess with that shit? Why would anyone do that? Why would my best mate screw around with my head
GETHIN	I don't understand
NICK	you do
GETHIN	I don't
NICK	you DO –
LORRAINE	do I?
GETHIN	I don't
NICK	you DO.
	YOU KNOW.
	You knew. You knew and you still went fucking blabbing on and on and on in my face
GETHIN	no
NICK	you've always known.
	So maybe you are. Like that. Maybe this is all some sick double bluff and you do think about those things. You're like that. Or you're in some kind of freaky denial. Completely nuts. How can we know?

GETHIN   it's me it's me

                It's *me*

                you know me

NICK   you know *me*

GETHIN   yeah I do

NICK   so –

                Why –

GETHIN   please

NICK   no. 'please.'

GETHIN   fuck. Fuck

NICK   fucken dick

LAYLA / SARAH /   fuck
TAYLOR'S MUM

                A breath.

                A breath.

GETHIN   I just thought he was weird

NICK   oh?

                A blink.

(LAYLA /   say it)
LORRAINE

GETHIN   I just thought

                I just thought he was, I don't know. I didn't
                know. I never thought about it

NICK   No?

GETHIN   it just, I just, put it away.

                I forgot.

NICK   Did you?

GETHIN   yeah

AUTHORITY	did I?
NICK	God that's really lucky. For you.
	I didn't.
	Beat.
GETHIN	I thought you – I thought he – liked you… more than me. That's all. I thought, he had that motorbike and he was letting you. It was so cool. I thought he let you ride it
NICK	shut the fuck up
GETHIN	I thought you were round there
NICK	SHUT up okay? You didn't, you liar you KNOW it – you didn't think that
GETHIN	we were only kids, Nick, I swear to God until you brought this up I never put it together – I never thought about it – I swear to God
NICK	I just don't believe you.
GETHIN	Never
NICK	How could you / not
GETHIN	I don't
NICK	How could you not – see
GETHIN	I never did
NICK	How? Don't you think it was weird he was showing us porn?
GETHIN	I don't know I don't know but I swear I didn't – or if
	… if I did… I didn't understand

TAYLOR'S MUM /   true.
LORRAINE /
AUTHORITY

Beat.

GETHIN	I didn't
NICK	mhm
GETHIN	…I forgot
NICK	right. Right.
GETHIN	you know?
SARAH / TAYLOR'S MUM	say sorry
NICK	That's why you suddenly just 'guessed'. Out of the blue.

Beat.

Still think he was cool?

GETHIN	fuck. Nick.

Rory –

NICK	DON'T say his name
GETHIN	okay
NICK	DON'T
GETHIN	okay
NICK	'cool'
GETHIN	I –
NICK	in my face. You're always in my face.

Hate to break it to you, Geth, but you're a dick sometimes.

GETHIN	(*Struggling to explain to himself.*) I… somehow didn't – connect
NICK	Don't.

I mean, he was showing us porn…

Beat.

GETHIN	you weren't…
NICK	I wasn't (*raped*)

but it was – it's enough. It's – it's not just
messin' about

/ (*Quiet*.) he had his cock out

OTHERS   (*Whisper*.) Rory was cool

/ didn't know

/ should've

/ say sorry

/ I love you

NICK   and your mum…

knows.

GETHIN, *stunned*.

(LORRAINE   sorry)

NICK   bitch

GETHIN   no she wouldn't… Nick… she couldn't

NICK   Shut up. For once. Why do you think he
fucked off so fast.

Silence.

GETHIN *sobs*.

NICK, *blank, looks almost relaxed. Exhales*.

GETHIN   I…

NICK   Is it in the genes. I always wondered, if your
dad / ever –

GETHIN   (*Small*.) No. Never.

He never… did anything.

NICK *absorbs. Nods. Lucky*.

I didn't think…

OTHERS   feel sick

GETHIN   I – didn't think…

OTHERS	exactly
GETHIN	(*Finally realising.*) I didn't think.
	I didn't think about you.
	GETHIN *places both trembling hands, palm down in front of him, without looking up.*
	A breath.
	He thinks about others.
	A thought, troubled.
	Is Sarah okay?
	NICK *nods, breathes.*
	GETHIN, *relieved, allows it to sink in.*
	Some moments.
GETHIN	Nick
NICK	What.
GETHIN	Do you have those files?
	NICK….
	GETHIN *breaks down, pulls it together again.*
	NICK *watches, unmoved.*
	Yeah.
	Yeah I do.
	You haven't even apologised
GETHIN	I'm sorry. Okay? I'm so sorry. Fuck the film. I didn't / mean…
NICK	okay.
	I don't give a fuck if you make your film.
	It's a great concept. Beats *Finding Nemo*. 'Finding Paedo' you should call it
GETHIN	fuck the film

NICK   Don't forget me when you're collecting your
                Sundance Award, shout out to Nick

GETHIN   Nick

                I'm not... a... I swear, I swear

NICK   Okay.

GETHIN   I'm sorry

OTHERS   sorry

LORRAINE   sorry

SARAH   love you

LAYLA   True.

AUTHORITY   You know.

NICK   Okay

                I know.

                (of course) I know you're not.

                Sorry. I just fucking wanted to kill you there.

                ...

                But it's cool. Now.

                I know...

                Right?

GETHIN   yeah.

                I am sorry.

                ...

                Okay.

                Thanks, mate.

NICK   no problem, mate.

                Neither look at the other.

                End.

A Nick Hern Book

Perve first published in Great Britain in 2011 as a paperback original
by Nick Hern Books Limited, The Glasshouse, 49a Goldhawk Road,
London W12 8QP, in association with the Abbey Theatre, Dublin

Reprinted 2012 (twice)

Perve copyright © 2011 Stacey Gregg

Cover image: Clare Lynch
Cover design: Ned Hoste, 2H

Typeset by Nick Hern Books, London
Printed in Great Britain by Mimeo Ltd, Cambridgeshire PE29 6XX

A CIP catalogue record for this book is available from the British Library

ISBN 978 1 84842 177 6